PROCRASTINATION

STOP PROCRASTINATING AND LAZINESS WITH THE HABIT OF DISCIPLINE

JONATHAN GREEN

DRAGON GOD BOOKS

Copyright © 2017 by Dragon God, Inc.

All rights reserved.

Simultaneously published in United States of America, the UK, India, Germany, France, Italy, Canada, Japan, Spain, and Brazil.

All right reserved. No part of this book may be reproduced in any form of by any other electronic or mechanical means – except in the case of brief quotations embedded in articles or reviews –without written permission from its author.

Influence and Persuasion has provided the most accurate information possible. Many of the techniques used in this book are from personal experiences. The author shall not be held liable for any damages resulting from use of this book.

Paperback ISBN-13: 978-1548781316

Paperback ISBN-10: 1548781312

Hardback ISBN: 978-1947667167

To my new bride

CONTENTS

Assessment Quiz — vii
Introduction — ix
Who Am I? — xi
About This Book — xiii

1. Are you a Procrastinator? — 1
2. How Serious of a Problem Can Procrastination Be? — 7
3. Causes of Procrastination — 15
4. Understanding and Harnessing Your Motivation — 29
5. What is Discipline? — 33
6. Goal Setting — 39
7. "Cheat" Your Way Out of Procrastination — 50
8. Health and Procrastination — 52
9. Your Physical Environment — 56
10. Meditation — 59
11. What Have We Learned? — 65

Take the Quiz — 67
About the Author — 69
Books by Jonathan Green — 73
One Last Thing — 75

ASSESSMENT QUIZ

Thank you for purchasing PROCRASTINATION.

As a special gift, I have a powerful procrastination assessment quiz for you.

This will help you to establish your exact procrastination baseline and allow to to track your progress.

Please use this analysis NOW and again after you finish the book.

https://servenomaster.com/procrastinate

INTRODUCTION

I have a lot of friends who brag about how well they operate under pressure. They can wait until the night before a test and cram everything they need to know in one massive coffee-fueled study session. They don't start working on a project until the clock is ticking.

But is this a skill that we want to harness?

You create a life with vast swaths of relaxation followed by moments of extreme stress and intensity. It's so much better to have a life where you never feel stressed out. Imagine how much easier life would be if you were always a week ahead of schedule - if you were always a month ahead on your rent instead of two weeks behind. Wouldn't that be something?

In my life, I have gone back and forth between being a great worker and a master of procrastination. I have been at both ends of the spectrum. This extensive experience has helped me see both sides of the coin, and I'm ready to walk you into the light. You don't have to feel stressed out or overwhelmed.

I have been self-employed since February of 2010. That's a long time to be in total, absolute control of your destiny. I have a wife and two children who rely on me to provide for them. That's a lot of pressure when you start getting behind. They are my primary motivation, but that's not nearly enough.

We all have reasons why we should finish projects and get ahead in life, but something stops us. It feels like there is this invisible force that keeps us from putting in the work that we need to do. You are reading this book, and that tells me everything that I need to know. You have the motivation to stop procrastinating. You know the projects that you want to get done in time.

If the problem isn't knowledge or motivation, what is it?

In this guide, I will take you on a journey start to the answer, and along the way, you might discover some things that surprise you.

WHO AM I?

My name is Jonathan Green, and I have been a full-time entrepreneur for seven years. I work for myself, and that means if I procrastinate, I won't have enough money to pay the bills. My ability to focus is what puts food on the table for my children.

You can find my entire business at ServeNoMaster.com. It is a site dedicated to helping people quit their jobs and making their dreams come true. A big part of that journey is the ability to start and complete projects.

I was the ultimate procrastinator when I was younger, and I suffered massively as certain points in my life. Procrastination cost me many fantastic opportunities and ruined my college graduation. Waiting until the last minute nearly destroyed me.

Now I'm able to focus in a way that most people can't imagine. I regularly write over twenty thousand words a day and have released dozens of bestsellers. But this book isn't about me; this is about taking you on a journey to unlock your true inner potential.

ABOUT THIS BOOK

By the end of this book, you will have a complete and total understanding of the nature and causes of procrastination. You will be able to diagnose the cause of your procrastination. Using that information, we will build a strategy together to remove procrastination from your life forever.

This book is the first in my new series, The Habit of Success. This book is intentionally shorter than the books in my Serve No Master series. The last thing I want to do is put a long book in front of someone struggling with procrastination. That would make it too easy for you to say, "This book is too long, maybe I'll read it tomorrow."

This book isn't just for people suffering from crippling procrastination. It's for anybody who would like to be a little more productive and accomplish a little more in their lives. Even increasing your efficiency by five percent can allow you to retire years early.

I want you to have the most amazing life possible. So let's go on a journey together and unlock your inner focus.

1
ARE YOU A PROCRASTINATOR?

When you were in school or college, did you ever find yourself up all the night studying the night before the exam? Or maybe writing an essay or report due the next morning? If you did, chances are good you regretted it when you were exhausted the next day!

At work, do you ever leave tasks to the last minute unnecessarily? Does this cause you extra stress? Do you become frustrated with yourself when you're always a step behind? Maybe you have trouble even understanding why you do this, even though you always have. And you probably always will.

We've all heard of the word "procrastination." The chances are that you have used it yourself, either describing yourself or others. Almost all of us, or perhaps absolutely all of us, have procrastinated about something on at least one occasion.

Unfortunately, procrastination is a very human fault, and it can sometimes seem like an unstoppable force. However, when procrastination becomes a habit and a consistent part of your life, there can be severe consequences. It can start to affect your grades, your income, and even your health. All those late-night, caffeine-fueled sessions are not good for your body.

We want to take action now before the problem gets any worse.

Procrastination is the practice of putting off important tasks that should be done right now, until "another time" or "another day." Have you ever said to yourself, "Why do today, what I can put off until tomorrow?" That's a common refrain for the perpetual procrastinator. We often think of procrastinators as lazy, but that's not quite right. Laziness and procrastination are different, and if we misdiagnose a problem, it becomes that much harder to find the cure.

A lazy person doesn't take action because they have no desire. They don't want to work harder or improve their lot in lives. Most lazy people spend their lives blaming other people for their lack of success and never put in any hard work.

A procrastinator wants a better life and wants to work harder, but for some reason (that we will cover shortly) cannot translate that motivation into action. If you didn't have any motivation, you wouldn't be reading this right now. Your problem is not laziness.

I have some good news. If you do have some vestiges hiding deep in your subconscious, the steps in this book that cure procrastination also help to cure laziness.

It's possible that your problem is not lack of focus, but instead focusing on the wrong thing. In this case, your problem is about prioritization, and it's one that I understand very well.

Planning My Day

I am currently working on multiple projects.

- Writing sales copy for three clients
- Finishing a new video course on Kindle books and marketing
- Traveling across the world for a conference next week
- Outlining, editing and planning several new books
- Creating a parenting emergency course
- Recording a series of videos for one of my publishers

I have a lot on my plate, and I can spend an entire day working on the wrong thing. Without a good strategy, I could spend the whole day working on a project that won't lead to profit for six months.

It's easy to look back on a day where you worked on the wrong thing all day and feel like you procrastinated when in reality you worked hard. You just worked hard on the wrong task.

Procrastination versus Prioritization: Characteristics

Characteristics of Procrastination

- You are procrastinating when you put off a task that should be done right now when there is **nothing more important or urgent** that needs to be done at this moment.
- Procrastination occurs when you do not get anything accomplished at a point when you should get something accomplished.

Characteristics of Prioritization

- You are prioritizing when you postpone a task because another task that is **genuinely more important and urgent** must take its place at the current moment.
- Prioritization occurs when you accomplish something that is more important or urgent than a task that you postponed.
- If you are **genuinely** tired and need rest or refreshment to be productive, then choosing to sleep or get refreshment first is a valid prioritization. Note that the word **"genuinely"** is key here!

Putting off a task without a solid plan is not prioritization. When you plan on taking care of something "later" but you don't really know what that means, then there is something wrong. Later can be in a few hours, tomorrow, or even in a few months. We want to get off this treadmill as quickly as possible.

When you are always putting things off until the last minute, you live in a perpetual state of agitation. There is always a deadline chasing you. It can feel like you're running down a mountain with a boulder rolling down after you. You don't deserve that feeling, and it's not a healthy way to live. Stress is one of the most sinister killers in our society, and the last thing you need is a life filled with easily avoidable stress.

I know what real stress is like and it's horrible. I went to the emergency room in my early thirties for a heart attack. I had so much stress from a bad business partnership that my stomach acid was eating through my esophagus behind my heart. I was so damaged that my esophagus began spasming and mimicked a heart attack. I'm lucky that it wasn't something worse, but seeing fear in a doctor's eyes in an emergency room is a moment I never want to repeat. And I certainly don't want that to happen to you.

Before we decide if you are a procrastinator, I have put together a little quiz for you. Procrastination is a habit, and that means we can fix the problem. We can replace bad habits with good ones and by the end of this book that's what we are going to do together. You probably already know if you're a procrastinator, but please take one minute to answer these questions to provide an objective baseline.

For this test to be accurate, you will have to make sure you think about each question carefully and be honest with yourself!

Test: Are You a Procrastinator?

1. How often do you go to bed feeling that you've accomplished everything of highest importance that you possibly could that day?
    a) Very rarely, or never.
    b) Often
2. Do you often decide to do tasks of lesser importance during time that should be devoted to tasks of greater importance?
    a) Yes

b) No, I never or rarely do this.

3. How do you tend to respond when faced with a task you find overwhelming?

a) I'm afraid I tend to put it off

b) I usually tackle it right away

4. Do you use "to do" lists?

a) Not usually, or never. Or if I do, I never stick with them.

b) Yes, I do, or sometimes do, and always stick with them.

Scoring: The greater number of "A" answers you chose, the more of a procrastinator you probably are.

Don't worry! By the end of this book, you will be armed with knowledge about procrastination, its causes, its effects, and the things you can do to break your procrastination habit!

I'm a big fan of the written word. And that means I love writing stuff down in the real world. Using computers and smartphones is fine, but our minds take things more seriously when we put pen to paper.

With that in mind, I would like you to start a "Stop Procrastination Journal." In this journal, you should complete the exercises and reflection questions set out in this book. The journal should take the form of an actual notebook, but if you absolutely, positively need to use a computer, then that's ok too. Start your journal by writing down your answers to these questions.

Then I would like you to write down the questions below and your answers. These reflections are important. If you are a procrastinator, you will be tempted to skip over them and promise to look at them 'later.' But please don't procrastinate when going through a book about procrastination.

If you are reading the paperback version of this book, you can write down your answers right in the book.

Reflections

1. What have you learned through reading this chapter? Take some

time to reflect on this question. What have you learned about yourself?

2. Have you been inspired to think of procrastination in a different way in any way than you did before?

3. How do you think that procrastination affects your life? How do you feel it has affected your life in the past, and how do you think it could have an impact on your life in the future if you do not get the habit under control?

4. Describe your determination to break your procrastination habit. How strong of a commitment are you ready to make?

Exercises

1. Think about the last time that procrastination affected you in a notably negative way, and answer the following questions:

a) What task was it that you put off doing?

b) Why do you think you put off doing it? What do you think might have been the cause or driver of your procrastination?

c) What were the exact consequences of your procrastination?

d) How did you feel about yourself when you realized what the consequences of your procrastination were? What were your feelings overall?

e) What lessons can you take from what happened here? Have you been successful in applying any of those lessons so far?

2

HOW SERIOUS OF A PROBLEM CAN PROCRASTINATION BE?

When we think of a procrastinator, we often think of a teenager lying on the sofa and watching television. Maybe that teenager on the couch is you, or maybe you see your own kids there now. As a father, I have started to notice that kids love to play and hate to work. I spend half my day asking my kids to pick up their toys and then just doing it myself.

Even though we think of procrastination as a childish problem, the long-term consequences can be quite serious. This harmful habit can exert severe, adverse effects on your life. It starts off as a small problem, but by the time you realize that's happening it can feel like the force of gravity.

Negative Effects that Procrastination Can Have on Your Life

1. Procrastination can prevent you from achieving your goals.

Each time you delay taking action, you push back the reward a little bit. It's like the frog that can only jump halfway to the door. He keeps hopping, but each hop is a little smaller than the last one and he never actually makes it through that door.

It's a problem that becomes more potent over time. Let's say that you procrastinated in high school and screwed around with some of your classes. You end up spending the summer taking the classes you missed or finishing those late projects. That stinks.

But what if you push things back even further and graduate at the end of summer. That doesn't seem like such a big deal, except that it pushes back when you can start college. So you start college in January after everyone else has had a whole semester to get to know each other. Your procrastination problem is still there, and it takes you five years to graduate instead of four.

That means you graduate eighteen months later than a nonprocrastinator. A small problem is snowballing into something serious. You start applying for jobs but you're older than the competition, so it takes a little longer to finally land that entry-level job. It doesn't help that you wait until the last minute to print your resume and that's the day the printer runs out of ink.

I don't want to go too far down this path because it only gets more and more depressing. You end up pushing back when you get married when you have kids and when you can finally retire. Procrastination can force you to work until the day you die. I don't want that for you.

The longer you put off doing important things, the much less likely it becomes that you will make meaningful accomplishments and reach your goals.

2. Procrastination can destroy your self-confidence.

We all use different scales to measure our confidence. Some people only care about money, some only care about looks, and some only care about popularity. As much as those elements can control how you feel about yourself, the real measure of your self-confidence is your ability to handle situations.

Firefighters have lots of confidence around fires because they have the training and expertise to handle that situation. The longer they spend in that job, the more that confidence sinks into their personality.

But imagine a firefighter who was always procrastinating. He had to take the fireman's test twice because he wasn't ready the first time. He's always the last one down the pole when the bell goes off, and sometimes he even gets left behind. How do you think that will affect his self-confidence?

A core element of self-confidence is your sense of self-efficacy (effectiveness as a person). If you don't feel effective as a person and you don't feel like you can handle things, your self-confidence will be paper-thin.

3. Procrastination can affect your self-esteem.

We use self-esteem and self-confidence interchangeably, but they don't mean the same thing. Self-esteem is a measure of how much we like, appreciate, and respect ourselves. How much you believe in yourself affects how much you like yourself, so the damage to your self-confidence caused by procrastination can start to hurt your self-esteem as well.

Being late and always under stress can damage your sense of self. Nobody wants to think of themselves as a procrastinator. There is no positive connotation for this word. It's always negative, and it makes us feel bad.

When you are always putting things off until the last moment, people stop relying on you. I have a few friends in my life that always show up late. When you ask someone like this what happened, they have a long explanation that boils down to them waiting until the last minute. They couldn't find their keys, or they needed to stop and get gas. Often, these people can't understand why they are always a step behind, but with a little perspective, we can see that this is a manifestation of their procrastination habit.

Procrastination can become so ingrained into your personality that people accept it as a part of who you are. But that simply leaves a permanent crack in your self-esteem, and it's time to repair it.

4. Procrastination can affect your education and training.

You may feel like the education phase of your life is complete. You never have to go back to college, and you certainly have no desire to repeat those teenage years. We all have the friend who brags that they don't know how to read anymore. The friend who reads one book a year and tells everyone about it like it's a great victory.

When we stop learning, we stop progressing in life. The person who reads one magazine article a year never gets the promotion and certainly never becomes the CEO. The inability to learn and grow will put a limit on every area of your life.

Also, extensive studies over the past twenty years have shown that procrastinators turn in lower quality work.[1] That lower quality work means lower grades and less benefit to those additional classes.

If you can't finish projects on time or show up to class when it's time to learn, you can put a glass ceiling on your career prospects....

5. Procrastination can affect your career.

It is easy to see how procrastination can have serious effects on the progress and success of your career. It is unlikely that your employer will be very happy if you procrastinate with important tasks. When you wait until the last minute to finish projects, your boss will think that you don't care that much about your job. You will be the first name to come up when it's time to downsize and the last name that comes up when it's time for promotions.

If you were the boss, who would you promote? Would you promote the person who comes in late to work and seems to have loads of free time right up until a project is due? Or would you promote the worker who keeps their head down and turns in each project two days early?

I run my own business, and I can tell you that no project stays the course. Every project I work on ends up changing somewhere along the way. When I'm working for a client, they often modify the vision for a project multiple times. I have worked on projects where something happened to the client, and they need to release workdays or even weeks early.

If your boss asks you about a project two days before it's due, they expect it to be eighty percent complete. Your boss doesn't want to hear that you haven't' started yet but not to worry because you are a master of operating under pressure. Those are not inspiring words.

6. Procrastination can cause you a lot of frustration and stress.

Operating under time pressure is the very definition of stress. Constantly wondering if tonight is the night you don't make that deadline. Nobody wants to live that way.

Do you remember when you procrastinated with assignments when you were in school or college? Do you recall how stressful it was the night before the due date, trying to make sure everything got done under the wire? And to get a decent grade, as well?

What's the first thing every student does after turning in that assignment just in time? They promise never to do it again. They promise to never put themselves through that much stress ever again because it's awful

It's time to start keeping that promise.

7. Procrastination can negatively affect your health.

Procrastination causes stress, and stress is bad for your health. There aren't too many steps in that logic chain. Stress is the cause of many awful diseases, including:[2]

- Heart disease
- Asthma
- Obesity
- Diabetes
- Headaches
- Depression
- Gastrointestinal

- Alzheimer's disease

We don't want any of these problems. Now I know that most of these diseases are long-term and they feel too far away to take seriously. But in the short term, procrastination cuts into your sleep. You spend late nights finishing projects and those late nights leave you feeling exhausted. Recent studies have shown

We have already established that procrastination causes excessive and unnecessary levels of stress. As you probably already know, stress is awful for human health and wellbeing. Stress contributes to a significant number of health problems, such as heart disease, high blood pressure, and a depressed immune system. Procrastination can also reduce the amount and quality of your sleep, which is also very bad for your health and wellbeing.

Recent studies have shown that drowsy driving is even worse than drunk driving![3] You need to get control of your rest again.

8. Procrastination will cause you to make very inefficient use of the time that you have.

Imagine how effective if you turned that eighteen-hour marathon session the night before a project is due, into just three hours of work per day for a week. You would get three more hours of work done, and you wouldn't need to guzzle all that coffee eating its way through your stomach lining right now.

Failure to plan is planning to fail.

We've often heard this quote that is attributed to Benjamin Franklin. When we don't plan out how we tackle a project, we use that time inefficiently. Can you imagine if the generals planning the Normandy invasion waited until the night before? We would all be speaking German today.

Large parts of my business success come from using time wisely. When you're always a step behind, that's no longer an option.

9. Procrastination can affect the recognition that you receive in your life.

What happens when you are late turning in that final college assignment? Something goes wrong, and suddenly there is an asterisk next to your name on the graduation form. You walk across the stage, and they give you an empty folder so you can "pretend" to graduate. This is awful, and it happened to me when I was twenty-one.

Even worse, at some schools, they don't let you walk across the stage at all. When you turn in work late, even if you manage to break the odds and do a good job, you are less likely to get awards and accolades. You do a great job, but your boss doesn't want to reward procrastination.

10. Procrastination can make you miss out on possible opportunities.

Procrastination can make you much more likely to miss out on opportunities. Often, it's the first person to raise their hand that gets the reward. The first person that says they want to go on the special trip gets that invite.

When you're in the back of the room trying to organize your presentation, you might not even hear your boss asking for volunteers to go to the conference in Hawaii.

Luck is opportunity meeting preparation.

Often attributed to Seneca, this quote is the reason that procrastinators feel unlucky. They are never prepared, so when opportunity comes calling, it ends up passing them by.

Reflections

1. Were you surprised by any of the potential negative effects of procrastination that you read about in this section? If so, why? If not, why not?

2. Now that you have read the list of negative effects that procrasti-

nation can have on your life, do you recognize any of them as already having already happened to you as a result of your procrastination?

3. Can you think of any additional negative effects that procrastination could have on your life?

4. Has reading this chapter lead you to make any new resolutions about your behavior? Has it made you more determined to break your habit of procrastination? Why or why not?

---

[1] HTTPS://WWW.PSYCHOLOGICALSCIENCE.ORG/OBSERVER/WHY-WAIT-THE-SCIENCE-BEHIND-PROCRASTINATION#.WLjRRhJ95E4

[2] http://www.webmd.com/balance/stress-management/features/10-fixable-stress-related-health-problems#1

[3] http://www.usatoday.com/story/news/2016/12/06/driving-5-hours-sleep-like-driving-drunk/94992718/

3

CAUSES OF PROCRASTINATION

There are multiple root causes for procrastination. In this chapter, we will work together to find that core problem. We want to do more than just attack the symptoms.

The causes of procrastination can be divided into two main categories: inner causes and outer causes. Together, we can unlock where your procrastination is starting and then nip this problem in the bud. Often, simply realizing the source of your procrastination makes it easy to solve.

When we don't know why we are procrastinating it can feel like the problem is in our DNA. But now it's time to shine a light on the real problem so we can begin the healing process. In this section, we will focus on isolating the cause of your procrastination, and as we move forward into the following chapters, we will move into our procrastination-busting strategies.

Internal Causes

1. You find the job unpleasant.

Sometimes you just don't want to do it. The greatest example of this is cleaning the bathroom. Nobody likes cleaning toilets, and that is why nearly every college student's bathroom is wretched. Distaste for the task leads us to put it off for as long as possible.

The problem with putting it off is that the problem only gets worse and worse. The longer you wait to clean that toilet, the more horrible the mess becomes.

One of the best ways to overcome this challenge is with gamification. You can create a game around the task or set up a reward system. When I was in college, my roommate dreaded cleaning the toilet above anything else. In exchange for my handling this dastardly task, he agreed to handle cleaning the kitchen and all the laundry.

Knowing the rewards for getting the job done turned the toilet into my favorite job. Twenty minutes of work saved me more than five hours every week.

You can save your favorite television show or a delicious snack for after you finish a particular task. The desire for that reward will help you to overcome your distaste for the job itself.

2. You are disorganized.

Sometimes the problem is just general disorganization. You know that you need to work on a task, but you have no idea how to handle it. When I get a job that I don't know how to complete, the desire to avoid that struggle causes me to put it off.

Let's look at physical disorganization first. Let's say you have guests coming over this weekend and you need to prepare the guest room, but the entire house is a mess. You don't know where to start first, so you end up putting off the task because of the unpleasant stress.

I remember hating cleaning my room in high school because it always became a monumental task that would take an entire day. Disorganization becomes a self-fulfilling prophecy. The longer you wait, the bigger the problem grows.

A common slip-up happens to people who try to cure their procrastination. You get so caught up the "organization" phase that nothing happens. You can spend hours changing the order of your to-do list but not do anything.

The most common feeling for the disorganized procrastinator is overwhelming. You feel like every task is so big that you just can't deal with it.

The first step in this process is to break big tasks into tiny pieces. Don't worry about the overall project. Just focus on cleaning the bathroom and only when that's done, will you think about your next task. This allows you to get a feeling of accomplishment each time you finish a small part of the overall task.

3. You feel overwhelmed.

You feel overwhelmed by the prospect of a task because it's so new. Sometimes the problem isn't disorganization. You can be very organized and then your boss rewards you with a project that is massively outside your experience and comfort zone. You simply have no idea what to do. What was meant to be a reward now feels like a curse?

The worst is when someone assigns you a complicated task like this and then refuses to provide guidance or answer questions. They feel like they are helping you by putting you through the crucible and maybe they are.

If breaking the task down into small pieces that you can handle isn't enough, the next tactic is to change your mindset. Whenever I see an obstacle in front of me, I see an opportunity for greatness. I focus on how good I will feel when I overcome. I think about the people who see this task and fail. Their failure will increase the value of my success. I love separating myself from the crowd.

Just changing how you think about that daunting task can make a huge difference.

4. You fear failure.

There is that moment that every child dreads. When a parent says to you, "I'm not angry; I'm disappointed." It's like a laser into your heart, and it makes you feel awful. Anger you can manage and deal with, but disappointment? That's a nightmare.

Failure is pretty fascinating. It's always worse in your mind than in is in real life. What we discover when we try something and fail is that it never lives up to our expectations. It's never as terrible as you think it will be. The fear is far more limiting than the failure.

When you fail at something, you can look around and wonder why you were ever that afraid. It's not nearly that bad, and you discover you have the strength to endure. You can rise up stronger because now you know that you can take a failure and survive.

Failure builds both character and confidence. You discover that you actually can handle those tough situations.

5. You fear success.

This seems counterintuitive, but this is the cause of procrastination for many people. Fear of success can take different forms. One of these is the fear that if you are successful, that people will expect you to be even more successful in other things and you will be a disappointment and embarrass yourself.

In another way, we fear that success will change us or cause the people around us to reject us. If you become rich, all your friends will abandon you. That's a real fear, and it's one of the primary reason people hit financial ceilings. A part of the subconscious fears success and thus fights against it.

The best way to deal with this fear is to take a long look in the mirror and be honest with yourself. You'll be surprised at what you discover when you finally speak honestly with yourself. Get your conscious and subconscious into alignment, and the sky is the limit!

6. You are a perfectionist.

When I was younger, the desire for perfection nearly killed me. I didn't want an A; I wanted that A+. I would spend so much time trying to get a perfect score in one class that I would suffer in other areas of my life. Life is about balance. As much as you want to do well intellectually, if you let your spirit or body suffer, all that work will have been a waste.

I finally decided that I would start doing work that was just "good enough." There is a point where more effort suffers from the law of diminishing returns. You can study three hours for a test and get an A or six hours and get an A+. Is doubling your study time worth a 2% increase? Often that time is wasted.

Spending those extra three hours sleeping, exercising or working on other projects will clear that logjam. When you start to realize that perfectionism is hurting you, you can unlock massive swaths of your time. That free time can be used to conquer the task that you didn't have time for before.

Last year, I launched my website ServeNoMaster.com, and the site was a disaster. It wasn't ready by any stretch of the imagination. There were broken links, missing videos and some pages didn't have perfect design. But the site was good enough. People enjoyed the content enough that they were willing to overlook the cosmetic problems.

The old me would have waited a full year to show anyone the site, and I would have lost so many fans and so much revenue. Find the right balance for you. It's better to get 80% of the project done than nothing at all.

7. You have poor decision-making skills.

Sometimes the problem is that you stink at making decisions. Indecisiveness is rampant in our society. We are in such fear of offending people that we are afraid to say the wrong thing. If we just don't make any decisions, then there is no risk of making a bad one.

If only that were true.

This is another area where I suffered when I was younger. I would always wait for other people to make decisions and I ended up seeing a lot of movies I hated that way. Following the crowd can work when you're in high school, but it leaves you a step behind later in life.

One of the main reasons many people join the military is to learn how to be decisive. It's better to make the wrong decision fast than the right decision too late. That's a tough concept to swallow at first. In the military, time is always a critical factor, so speed to decision becomes critical.

An excellent way to deal with poor decision-making skills is to go outside your comfort zone. Find a hobby or activity that requires constant quick decisions. It can be anything from street chess to snowboarding. Any activity with a time element will help you sharpen this skill.

8. You somehow hope that the task will go away.

The children of the wealthy often become lazy procrastinators because they have no challenges in life. If they avoid doing something long enough, their parents just pay someone to take care of it for them. I knew a very wealthy kid in high school who tried to buy the DMV when he failed his driver's test.

Struggle is what hones greatness, and as a parent, it can be difficult to find that balance. I want my children to have amazing lives, but I also want them to be strong.

If your parents helped you every time you faced a problem when you were younger, they did you no favors. You have to learn to fill in the gap now and make up for that carefree childhood. I didn't learn how to stop procrastinating and run a business until my parents cut me off. Only when I knew that there was no help coming from mommy and daddy did I unlock my true potential.

Start seeing challenges and obstacles as opportunities for greatness and you will look forward to these challenging tasks.

9. You resent the task in some way.

I would clean my room if my mom had asked me, but since it was my sister, there's no way I'm doing it. She's not the boss of me!

It sounds childish but admit it; sometimes you don't want to do something at work because the wrong person gives you the task. You don't want to accept an assignment from a coworker because it lowers your political position.

I get that. This isn't a book about office politics, so you'll have to navigate those waters yourself for now. I cover networking and office politics a great deal in some of my others books, but for procrastination, the key is to separate the task from the emotion.

Sometimes you just have to do it.

10. You hope the task will somehow be easier to carry out at a later time.

I am still waiting for talk-to-type technology to achieve perfection so that I can write books without touching a keyboard. I have been waiting for this panacea for more than two decades, and I still don't think we're close. I might have to wait a couple more decades.

If that were my excuse for inaction, I would lose fifty years of my life to procrastination.

We sometimes put off a task hoping that technology or someone else will fill in the gap. You're just passing the buck, and it's time to admit that waiting always makes a job harder, not easier.

Without absolute objective proof that the task will be easier if you wait, you must reject this idea.

11. You find the task boring.

I've never found that waiting to do something makes it less annoying. Instead, you get to suffer from the anticipation of boredom before you enjoy it. It's far better to get through the boredom and get to what you would rather be doing.

It is critical that you place rewards after you complete your tasks, rather than before them. Eating ice cream before dinner never motivated anyone to eat their vegetables.

12. You lack motivation.

When the task itself provides you with no motivation, the best solution is to generate motivation from an external source. (Give yourself a reward when you finish.)

13. Your energy level is low.

If your mental or physical energy level is low, you will probably be more likely to procrastinate. Stress and anxiety can melt away your mental and physical energy. As an entrepreneur, every area of my life is my total responsibility. If I don't take care of my body, then my mental faculties will suffer.

Taking care of your body is critical. If I go three days without exercise, my work quality suffers dramatically. I always have some yoga routines on my computer so I can exercise whenever I need too.

If you have a bad diet, your body has to spend extra energy trying to process that garbage. When I eat fried food, even though it tastes delicious, my body becomes lethargic. Your diet and exercise regime may be the source of your procrastination.

14. You have problems focusing.

If you have problems focusing, you might be more likely to procrastinate. Difficulty focusing might cause you lots of frustration, and make you more likely to want to put off having to face the problem.

I'm terrible at focusing. To stay on task, I had to train myself through repetition. There are so many fun ways to lose focus these days. You can watch a movie, read some email, or even look for a date in less than five seconds. The Internet is a powerful force, and it is a great distractor.

If you don't need to be online, consider unplugging that router. Try to eliminate the causes of your distraction and focus becomes much easier.

15. You have poor prioritization skills.

If you have poor prioritization skills, you are more likely to procrastinate. Sometimes you have to choose between the task you want to do and the task you should.

A sign that this is your problem is a garage filled with gear from hobbies you never completed. If you start a new hobby every few weeks, that's a bad sign. Do you have ten half-finished novels sitting in your desk drawer?

Starting projects is the fun part. Finishing them is the hard part.

This is where people often decide to hire a life coach. They pay someone else just to help them organize their schedule. You can try one of the many free task managers online. Many of them let you assign a weighted value to each task. You can then prioritize your day, and this tool helps bridge the gap for you.

16. You're not thinking long-term.

If you have trouble thinking long-term, you might be more likely to procrastinate. If a week from now, or a month from now, or a year from now seems like an incredibly vague prospect, you are more likely to put off tasks until some seemingly indefinable time.

I wrote the book 20K in a Day to help writers shorten the distance between the start and end of a project. The faster you can write a book, the closer that final goal is. When a book is nine months from completion, it's hard to take it seriously.

This book is a new exercise for me. I'm trying to write this entire book in a single day and believe me, there are plenty of distractions coming my way, but we still have lots of ground to cover together!

When you set your goals correctly, with a fixed measurement and a timeframe, you can then break that time into smaller pieces. Take a month-long task and break it into thirty daily tasks. And take each day and break it into five smaller tasks.

Instead of some vague, far-away goal, you can focus on just your tasks for today.

External Causes

There are three primary sources for external distractions. There are fun things you want to do. People you want to do fun things with. And the almighty distraction that comes from within your computer.

We can block these procrastination-causers by setting up proper infrastructure in your life.

1. General distractions.

We live in a fast and modern world where distractions are a heartbeat away. If you work from home, you can walk across the room to turn on the television, fire up your stereo or make a phone call. Smartphones are now filled with meaningless apps and games that do nothing other than sucking the money out of your bank account.

When you work at an office, a fun coworker at the desk next to you can be all it takes to keep you from doing any work. Why work on the Henderson account when you could be listening to a hilarious story about Sally from accounting?

Many offices have loads of meetings just so that middle managers can avoid doing any actual work. Meetings are how many companies procrastinate while pretending to be productive. When I was a volunteer working in my early twenties, I once attended an eight-hour meeting discussing what game we would play for the opening three minutes of a presentation the next day. It was an incredible waste of time that my coworkers justified just by using the word meeting.

The way to deal with these distractions is to change your physical location. If you get distracted at home, work in a cafe. If you get distracted working on coffee shops, go to the library. If you spend all your time at work talking to people instead of doing any actual work move your desk. Ask your boss to change your cubicle so that you can be more productive again.

Simply isolating the cause of your procrastination and distraction will make it easier for you to shift your behavior.

2. You are influenced by people around you.

In this case, people around you are actively working to sabotage you. They will never admit it, but some of your friends, roommates, and loved ones may be the reason you never get anything done. You might have roommates who always distract you when you're working and suggest watching a movie or going to a bar. You might have family members who want to play with you when you need to finish your work.

They are not malicious, but they sure know how to distract you. Who wouldn't rather watch a movie than grind on a boring project?

When I'm writing, I can get in the absolute zone, but if my concentration gets broken, it can be tough to get it back.

Even worse are the people around you who procrastinate and try to get you to join them. There are the kids who hang out together after school and do anything other than study. If one child from the group decides to get serious and do his homework on time, they make fun of him. They use social pressure to keep him from putting in the work to improve his lot in life.

If you have people like this in your life, the first step is to explain to them that you need to get work done. When you are working on something important, put a sock on the door or wear a particular set of headphones. Put up a signal to block people accidentally distracting you.

For the people who can't be stopped by these actions, sit down and have a talk with them. Explain why you are trying to get more work done and how you want to have a better life. Explain that it's about your life and not about you rejecting them in any way. If they care about you, they will understand and give you the time you need to get your tasks done early.

You may need to isolate some of your friends. I have a few friends that I never spend time with when I have a project I'm working on. They are my "fun time friends, " and I spend time with them after I have earned it. I have turned them into my reward for finishing a dreaded task.

3. You are distracted by your computer.

Social media, Google, and email are massive sources of distractions. There are so many ways that your computer can distract you, that I will have to create a separate book on this topic. The average office worker spends more than six hours a day checking email.[1] That's a whole lot of not working!

We all have our distractions. If you have a game on your computer, uninstall it. If the Internet distracts you, turn off your Wi-Fi. There are loads of amazing apps and programs designed to help you focus. Some great writing programs block access to the rest of your software until you hit your word count goal. Talk about motivation!

It's easy to let your computer become a place for entertainment rather than a tool for productivity. Start purging all the unnecessary distractions from your computer and your procrastination will fade away.

Reflections

1. Now that you have carefully read and thought about all the different causes of procrastination, which of the causes do you feel most strongly affect your life?

2. Which of the causes discussed in this chapter do you feel most strongly apply to you?

3. Which is the single most significant cause of procrastination in your life? If you have multiple causes, add them to your journal and rank them by how much each cause affects you.

4. What other insights have you reached in this chapter about your procrastination?

5. While reading this chapter, what thoughts did you have regarding steps you could take to fight your procrastination habit?

6. Discuss any additional thoughts you have had about the importance of motivation while reading this chapter.

Exercises

Exercise 1

You should complete this exercise in your Stop Procrastination Journal.

For at least two of the causes of procrastination listed above, write a scenario or story in which this factor is causing procrastination. The person in the story can be yourself, someone you know, or an imaginary person or character. Make sure that you clearly define the task and the source of procrastination.

Exercise 2

You should complete this exercise in your Stop Procrastination Journal.

Choose two causes of procrastination (different than the ones you chose in the first exercise). Below, you will find a list of tasks and scenarios. For at least ten of these, write how you could combat the two causes of procrastination you have chosen for this exercise.

If you wish to go the extra mile, you can choose two different answers for each of the scenarios. Make sure to choose causes that you think are likely.

(For example, with task one you would write about trying to finish a computer course when your college roommate wants to go to a party and your friends keep messaging you on Facebook about the same party.)

- Writing an important paper for a university course.

- Writing a report for work.
- Planning a birthday party for a family member.
- Planning for an important presentation at work.
- Preparing for a job interview.
- Planning a vacation.
- Going grocery shopping.
- Cleaning your home.
- Organizing your desk.
- Reading a book.
- Writing a difficult email or letter.
- Writing a report for work.
- Revising your resume.
- Booking a doctor's appointment.
- Speaking to your manager at work about a problem.

---

[1] http://www.huffingtonpost.com/entry/check-work-email-hours-survey_us_55ddd168e4b0a40aa3ace672

4

UNDERSTANDING AND HARNESSING YOUR MOTIVATION

The fight against procrastination starts with harnessing your motivation. Without that motivation, you would be lazy rather than a procrastinator. Buying (or stealing) this book and reading it is a sign that you have some motivation. That small spark of motivation is enough for us to work together to create the inferno that is within you.

Inherent Motivation

Let's isolate the core of your motivation together and use that as the key to breaking through your procrastination barrier. (I'm happy to use multiple metaphors to get you motivated!)

Every task before you comes with an intrinsic motivation. That motivation might be to:

- Impress a date with your clean house
- Get your roommate to do their chores
- Keep your job
- Get a passing grade
- Graduate college or high school

- Get in shape
- Live longer

There are loads of reasons tied to each task that you've been putting off. But if this built-in motivation were enough, you wouldn't be stuck where you are right now.

Motivation Exercise

Sometimes the motivation is broad (like keeping your job) and sometimes it's very specific (like impressing your date tonight.) It's time to crack open your journal again.

Write down a list of the times you are most guilty of procrastination. With each of these tasks that you like to avoid, isolate the motivation for that task. We are going to make a list of motivations that aren't quite getting the job done yet.

I have put together some questions to help you with this task. Write your answers in your Stop Procrastination Journal.

1. What is your motivation? Do you have more than one motivation? If so, which of these motivations do you feel is the most important? Why? Why are the other ones relevant, as well?

2. Brainstorm on the reasons why completing this task is essential to your success.

If you do not feel sure that you even have a motivation to do the job required, you need to dig a little deeper; trying to complete a task without any motivation at all is tough.

For tasks for which you do not immediately find any apparent motivation, ask yourself the following questions. They will help achieve a better idea of what your motivation is or should be.

1. What is the reason you have to carry out this task?

2. What led to your having the responsibility of carrying out this task?

3. How will you be rewarded if you complete this task successfully? What will happen if you do not finish this task successfully?

4. How would not completing this assignment hold you back from success in an area or areas of your life, however small you think they might be?

Reward Yourself

A strong sense of motivation will help you stay on track and keep your focus. It will make you less susceptible to the allure of distractions, and to other less important tasks that you might want to use as an excuse for putting off the more important one at hand.

When a task doesn't have enough motivation to bring you to action, look for ways to add in additional motivation. Create a reward system that works for you. When you finish a dreaded task, allow yourself to watch your guilty pleasure television show.

One of my great distractions and pleasures is video games. I don't have any video games on my computer because I know that would murder my productivity. Instead, I only buy a new game or allow myself to play after I've earned it. I turn my distraction into a reward for getting the task done.

Adding external motivation is often all it takes to push you out of the procrastination zone.

Creating your own incentive is effective precisely because you are the one who chose it. You know yourself far better than I do.

Reflections

Record your thoughts on these reflection questions in your Stop Procrastination Journal.

. . .

1. Think about some occasions in the past where a lack of motivation caused you to procrastinate. Did you realize that it was a lack of motivation that was driving your procrastination at the time? Why or why not?

2. How do you think that better knowledge about how to identify and focus on your motivation will help you in breaking your habit of procrastination?

3. Did the questions in the previous sections of this chapter give you a better idea of how to discern and focus on your motivations for tasks?

4. What rewards can you do to push your motivation over the top and get your tasks done?

5

WHAT IS DISCIPLINE?

We all have a general idea that self-discipline helps us to get the job done. But have you ever thought about what that word means? Why do some people have discipline while others have none? Is it nature or nurture? Is it possible to improve your discipline?

When a child lacks discipline, you can send them to military school to fix the problem. Is there an option for adults? (Other than joining the army.)

Discipline is the opposite of procrastination and the more discipline you bring into your life, the easier conquering your procrastination demon will become.

We often use the words self-discipline and willpower interchangeably. But if they were the same thing they wouldn't have different names.

What is willpower? Willpower is the ability to do something you need to do because you are determined to, regardless of any thoughts, emotions, or desires that come into your mind.

Self-discipline is essential to the exercise of willpower. It is your ability to understand and control yourself in sophisticated ways. Self-discipline usually involves restraint, capacity to refrain from doing something when you shouldn't do it, and the ability to apply yourself when you need to do so.

Willpower is your desire to change your procrastinating ways, and self-discipline is how we can measure your success.

We know that discipline is good. But how much discipline do you have? The term is so vague as to be unusable. For that reason, I created a test to help you measure your current discipline level.

Below is a test that will help give you an idea of your current level of self-discipline. A low score on this test is not a sign that your life is always going to be terrible. Instead, it shows you areas for improvement, and that should get you very excited!

Whenever someone points out an area of weakness in my life, I see it as a chance to improve and turn that weakness into a strength. It is far better to know about a weakness than to be unaware.

Self-Discipline Test

1. If you don't feel like doing something you need to do, how good are you at forcing yourself to do it?
    a) Not very good
    b) Reasonably good
    c) Good
    D) Very good

2. If you need to refrain from doing something that you want to do, how good are you at practicing that restraint?
    a) It's a struggle.
    b) I can stop myself
    C) It is so easy that I don't even think about it

3. How good are you at consistently carrying out activities you need to do to achieve major goals? An example of this might be working out to improve your health.
    a) I'm not good at this.
    b) I am good at this.

Scoring: The greater number of "A" answers you chose, the lower your level of self-discipline. But don't worry! We will discuss ways that you can take action to improve your skills of self-discipline.

Ways to Improve Your Level of Self-Discipline

1. Fake it til you make it

This seems like a trite piece of advice, so let's break it down into something manageable and actionable. Break out your journal and write down a description of the person that you wish you were. Give this person a different name than you. I might call this ideal or improved version of myself Jonathan 2.0.

Jonathan 2.0 has great discipline. He always eats healthy and starts every day by working out. He finishes his tasks on time and only after getting his work done does he let loose.

A little description like that in your notebook is enough to get you started. Whenever you feel your discipline slipping, you can just say, "What would Jonathan 2.0 do in this situation?" (Obviously, replace my name with your own!)

The more time you spend pretending to be the 2.0 version of yourself, the sooner you will turn into this person. This exercise also works for increasing your confidence.

2. Create routine

The more structure you build into your day, the easier it is to maintain your discipline. I work for myself and live on a tropical island. I can get up whenever I want to.

I have a friend who lives this way. He sleeps in every day til mid-afternoon. He doesn't get up at a particular time, but just lets his body tell him when it's time to get up. He has no set list of tasks when he starts working, so I never know what he'll be working on when I speak to him. He is always behind on projects.

The lack of routine leaks from his personal life into his professional. This happens to the best of us. When I was getting up in the afternoon, the quality of my work was inferior. Adding structure into my day has made life easier, and my productivity has skyrocketed.

I get up every morning at the same time and start my day with the same tasks. Anytime I miss my morning routine, the rest of my day slips off the tracks.

Whether you have a boss or not, insert as much routine and structure into your day as possible. I know that we all have a rebellious streak. Why work for myself if I am going to have a curfew? You probably want to shout that from the roof right now.

But routine and structure have value. Look at that experiment every high school student tries when you take away their bedtime. They think it's awesome to stay up all night doing what they want, but the next day at school is a total drag. Anarchy isn't always a good thing.

Structure helps to build discipline.

3. Pay attention to your health

I can't say this enough. When I go three days without working out my personality tanks, and I start to get depressed. Your body is a machine, and when you don't take care of it, it loses efficiency. Would you put sugar in your car's gas tank? So why do you put it in yours?

This might feel like a Catch-22. You need to exercise to have discipline, but exercise is the very activity you need the discipline to do.

Here is the ultimate secret. Find a sport you like. Going to the gym or watching workout videos will always feel like a job. But going to the park to play soccer sounds like fun. Everyone has a different sport. Right now mine is surfing. I enjoy every single second I'm on the water, but when I get back home every muscle in my body aches. It's a tough workout.

Find a sport that you enjoy, and this process turns a chore into a pleasure.

. . .

4. Be kind and fair to yourself

People who set up strict rules and leave no room for failure always end up failing. The person who starts a diet assuming that they will make no slip ups is the one who collapses after one cookie.

Making brittle rules ensures that you never succeed. Never start a plan with the assumption that there will be no trials and tribulations. Expect struggles and focus on learning from them.

When your discipline lapses, don't waste time punishing yourself. Forgive yourself, and move on immediately. There is no point wasting time crying over spilled milk. The best thing you can do with your mistakes is to learn from them.

5. Reward yourself

Find ways of rewarding yourself for meeting self-discipline goals.

6. Give yourself credit where it is due!

When you are successful in your self-discipline efforts, acknowledge it and make sure to congratulate yourself!

7. Meditation

Meditation can be extremely useful in improving your capacity for self-discipline. The entire practice of mediation is built upon discipline. You have to set aside the time to meditate and then hold still while you are doing it. Adding a few minutes of meditation to your day can help your mind stay focused.

Reflections

1. How strong do you think your self-discipline is right now? Why?
2. How do you feel that improving your self-discipline could help you fight your habit of procrastination?
3. What did you think about the list of techniques for improving

your self-discipline set out in this chapter? Which of them do you think will be most helpful? Did any surprise you? If so, why?

4. Can you think of additional techniques that aren't on this list?

Exercise

On two occasions (one week and two weeks after implementing the techniques set out in this chapter into practice), answer the questions below in your Stop Procrastination Journal.

1. Do you feel that your self-discipline level has improved? How much do you feel it has improved? If it hasn't improved, why do you think this might be? What do you think you could do to rectify this situation?

2. Which of the tips for improving self-discipline set out in this chapter did you find most effective for you? Which of them did you find least effective?

3. What will be your next step in your quest for better self-discipline? Will you continue as you have been doing, or will you make any changes?

4. Do you feel that improving your discipline has made it easier to resist the temptation to procrastinate?

5. Has developing your self-discipline changed your self-confidence and self-esteem levels?

6. How has improving your self-discipline affected other areas of your life?

7. Did implementing these techniques change your opinion on the state of your self-discipline before? Were you less self-disciplined than you thought?

8. Have any of the ideas you had about self-discipline and its impact on your life and success before reading this chapter changed? How?

6

GOAL SETTING

Proper goal setting is one of the most important things you can do to help break your habit of procrastination. Good goal setting consists of the setting of **achievable** goals. Setting non-achievable goals is pointless, and will just cause frustration and more procrastination.

Setting goals correctly is a crucial step in the war against procrastination for three reasons:

1. When you achieve one of your goals, you gain a feeling of confidence.
Better confidence in your abilities will make you less likely to put things off in fear of failure.

2. Goal setting will help you better organize your time, and improve your prioritization skills.
When you set clear goals, you will feel and be more organized. You will be better able to prioritize.

. . .

3. Goals help you organize your schedule.

A properly set goal has a timeline and a way to measure success. You can then divide the target into daily pieces. If you want to lose thirty pounds in thirty days, you know that you need to lose one pound every day to hit your goal.

A good goal turns a big task into a series of manageable, smaller tasks. As you hit each small goal, you can feel actual progress. As a writer, my world is defined by word counts. Each time I hit a daily goal on the path to finishing a new book, I can feel a measurable sense of accomplishment.

The more feelings of accomplishment you can put between you and a goal, the more likely you are to achieve it.

Goal Setting Test

How good are your goal-setting skills right now? This test will help us find out together.

1. Do you write out your goals and develop plans for how to achieve them?

   a) Yes, I do sometimes or all the time.

   b) No, not usually, or only rarely.

2. Do you think about large goals or do you immediately look for ways to break that goal into smaller pieces?

   a) I look to break my goals into manageable chunks as quickly as possible.

   b) When I get a new goal, I usually feel overwhelmed by how large the task is.

3. How good would you say you are at prioritization?

   a) I think I'm quite good at it, or very good at it.

   b) I don't think I'm very strong at this.

Scoring: The more "A" answers you have, the better your goal-setting skills. If you had more "b" answers, your goal-setting skills need a little more fine-tuning. But don't worry! You will learn about how to improve your goal-setting skills right now.

What is a Goal?

This is crucial, so please focus especially hard for the next two minutes.

A goal MUST have a way to measure success and a due date. If you have a goal without these two elements, you don't have a goal.

I WANT to lose weight is a desire.

I AM GOING to lose weight is a dream.

I AM GOING to lose ten pounds in the next thirty days is a goal.

YOU NEED a specific goal and a specific date.

Why is Setting a Schedule Important?

Setting a schedule and using to-do lists are very helpful in keeping you organized, and ensuring you use your time efficiently.

Schedules and to-do lists can take several different forms and depend on what you find most useful. You may need to dabble with several formats to find what works best for you.

You may work better with lists or advanced project management software. Most of the expensive project management programs let you sign up for free if you don't have a team. They only start charging when you begin to collaborate. Since you will never need to do that, you can use some very powerful tools for free.

Only through experimentation will you find the best tool for you.

You might find that you hate software and instead, you start carrying around a physical planner. If that works for you, then implement it.

As you being to improve your organization, keep schedules and deadlines separate; they are not interchangeable terms. The deadline for a project is just another name for a goal. Usually, a deadline is a goal that someone else has set for you.

Your schedule will be the goals, steps and smaller tasks that you need to complete on the way to this deadline, combined with a timeline.

Let's say a student has an essay due on May 30th. That day is their deadline.

A good student will use that deadline to build out a schedule. This plan will combine all the tasks needed to complete the essay and attach smaller deadlines to them. The essay starts with choosing a topic. Once they complete this task, they go into the research phase. Then they write the first draft. Then the final draft. Then it's time to organize all the sources and ensure that they are in the proper format. Finally, it's time to turn in that essay.

If we just make a list of these tasks, that is a significant step forward, but it's not a schedule. The student has two days to choose a topic, ten days to research, five days for the first draft and so on. Now we have the makings of a schedule!

Using a schedule allows you to block out enough time to finish a project without needing to cram all the work in at the last minute with marathon writing sessions at the library the night before the essay is due.

Below are some exercises that will help improve your schedule setting skills. Like all other exercises in this book, make sure to write your answers in your Stop Procrastination Journal.

Schedule Setting Exercise

1. Think of a real goal that you want to achieve. Write down this goal clearly in your Stop Procrastination journal. Let your entry take this form:

"Goal: _____due on _____", and put this at the top of the page.

How can you measure the success of this goal? What is the exact date you need to achieve this goal by?

2. Write a detailed and orderly list of smaller tasks that you will have to complete to achieve your goal. Break these tasks into the smallest pieces possible.

3. Take each of these micro-tasks and write down how long they will take. Each of these little tasks should be measured in hours, not days.

Your big job is now a series of smaller tasks that you can easily check off your list. You can also fill out a schedule to know exactly what you will be working on next Tuesday.

Can you start to feel like you are in control of your life again?

Daily Schedule Setting Exercise

Let's practice making a daily schedule together. You can use your work from the previous exercise or just create an imaginary goal. This is just practice.

Depending on your work and family situation, you may already have a pretty full schedule. Certain events happen every day. I get up every morning at 5 AM to record 1-2 podcast episodes. At 6 AM, I wake up my wife and children to do an exercise video together. We usually do yoga or kettlebells and are finished by 7 AM. Every day at my house starts like this.

Start your practice schedule by including all the recurring events. When do you get up, eat breakfast and drive the kids to school? Then add in all of your meetings and appointments. Now you can start filling in the rest of the day with imaginary events, or even better, tasks from the previous exercise.

Your schedule should be chronological. Please write down at least one full day in your Stop Procrastination Journal.

Additionally, this might be a very good time to check out some of the software and tools you can use to organize and schedule your days at ServeNoMaster.com/Procrastinate.

To-Do Lists

What about to-do lists? Are they helpful? Yes, they certainly are! To-do lists tend to be more informal, but they can be put together more quickly. Also, the tasks listed in them do not need to be in a specific order. To-do lists can be particularly helpful in making you feel calmer and more control in anticipation of a day that is still a bit uncertain, but that you know will be busy.

I tend to use to-do lists when I'm traveling or shopping. Just yesterday I was at a mall for the first time in over six months. I use the list app on my phone to write down all the purchases that I needed to make. Rather than listing the items by store, I listed them as I thought of them.

As I walked around the mall, I could check my list and get everything I needed, based on which stores I was walking past. It's a little looser than a schedule, but it's more useful in this type of situation.

I also use to-do lists a lot for big projects. Certain projects have steps that always repeat, such as building a membership area or designing a book cover. Because these tasks repeat, I can copy and paste them from one project to the next. I never put a timeline on a book cover, because it's impossible to predict. Some covers only take two days to design, and others can take an entire month. It depends on the artists I work with and how quickly they unlock my vision.

Let's do a little practice together now.

To-Do List Exercise

Write a to-do list for a day coming up soon in your Stop Procrastination Journal.

Make a list of all the things you want to do tomorrow or this weekend. Try this looser format and see if it works better for you.

Micro-Tasks

When the feeling of a task being overwhelming is making you more likely to procrastinate, it can be extremely helpful to break the task down into "micro-tasks." These are the smaller tasks or steps that you need to take to complete a larger task.

If you've read any of my other books, you know that I'm obsessed with breaking any project down into the smallest tasks possible. This book is shorter than my other books, but it's still broken down into nearly one hundred sections. I love slicing my work up!

Let's take a moment to look at a task from the past where procrastination reared its ugly head and see if implementing micro-tasks would have helped you.

Micro-Tasks Exercise

1. When was the last time procrastination bit you? A task that was overwhelming. It might be the exact reason you grabbed this book.

Take that daunting task and break it into the smallest pieces possible. Even if you have to spend an hour with your journal, this exercise is worth the time investment. When you have that task broken down into small pieces, take a moment to assess your emotions.

Does the task feel as daunting now? Does it feel more manageable? Can you see how breaking down this task could have helped you back then?

2. Let's try it for a real project in your future. Do you have an upcoming project? Are you thinking of writing a book? Start by breaking that project into pieces.

Once you have written all the tasks you need to complete as part of this project, place them in order. Some tasks can be tackled at the same time, but others must be done in the correct order. You can't design the cover for a physical book until you have a final page count.

The page count determines the thickness of the spine. But for a digital book, you can design the cover while you are writing the book.

Organize your tasks and see how much easier the thought of writing that novel feels now.

Reflection on the Micro-Task Approach

Do you feel that using the micro-task method could help you tackle those tasks you have been putting off?

Do you see how breaking tasks into smaller pieces makes them feel more manageable and takes away that feeling of being overwhelmed?

Reward Yourself!

Find ways to reward yourself when you complete tasks and micro-tasks. There are plenty of great ways to reward yourself, just make sure that the reward fits the scale of the accomplishment. Don't buy yourself a car just for choosing the title of your next book!

You probably don't need me to help you think of ways to reward yourself, but here are a few reward ideas to get your mind warmed up:

- Listening to some new music
- Watching a movie
- Watching a television show
- Watching a YouTube video
- Reading the next chapter of a novel
- Reading a magazine
- Buying a small treat
- Purchasing something you have wanted for a long time
- Going on a special trip
- Eating a snack you especially like

The Significance of Self-Confidence

As I've already touched upon, self-confidence is a crucial ingredient in the fight against procrastination. Self-confidence plays a significant role in goal setting.

Here are a few reflections to deepen your understanding of this connection. Make sure to keep your Stop Procrastination Journal handy.

Reflections

1. Has a lack of self-confidence ever been a cause of your procrastination? Think about this carefully. Write down a time when you put off working on a task because you didn't believe that you were up to the job. This doesn't just have to be a task you put off; it can also be something you quit. Was there something you gave up on because you didn't think you had the chops?

2. Do you think that confident people procrastinate? How does the confident "You 2.0" handle intimidating tasks? Does version 2 think of reasons to quit or put off the work or does this future version of you savor the opportunity to overcome?

3. Can you see how increasing your confidence (or even faking it) can help you to overcome the desire to procrastinate?

Achieving a State of Flow

It's time to get into the zone. Some people prefer to call this a state of flow or even "getting into state." Either way, it is when you are totally focused on the task at hand, and you ignore the world around you. This is the dream state that many people seek but struggle to find.

How can someone achieve this zenlike state of absolute focus consistently? If you're a writer, then I can't recommend reading my other book *20K a Day* enough. The section on ritual will help you achieve the zone every single time you sit down to write.

For different tasks, we need to take different approaches to getting into the zone. Here are a few tips that will help you find that perfect formula for you:

1. Clearly identify your goals.

How can you get in the zone if you don't know what you are trying to achieve? I set a new goal in front of me every day, and the desire to complete that primary daily task helps me stay focused.

It's also important to know why you want to achieve that goal. Without the 'why', it's hard to stay motivated.

2. Avoid interruptions.

Do everything you can to avoid being interrupted. No matter what you may have heard, multitasking is an abysmal failure. Every single study of the process has found that it's a productivity killer.[1]

All it takes is one person walking into the room to ask you a meaningless question to kick you out of the zone. Makes sure that's not going to happen. Lock the door, put on your special headphones or tape a message to your back. Do whatever it takes.

3. Focus on Process

I'm playing a game with myself today. I want to see if I can write an entire twenty thousand word book in a single day. It's a daunting challenge, and I could easily overwhelm myself. At least three times today I thought about slowing down and just trying to finish over a weekend. But that wasn't my original goal.

Rather than focus on finishing the entire book, I'm just writing one little section at a time. This book isn't twenty thousand words right now. It's forty 500-word sections. I am only looking to hit that next little goal, and this keeps me totally dialed into the process.

4. Plan Your Steps

Don't skip the rest of this chapter. You need to have a list or schedule ready before you start a project. If you are in the middle of the zone and suddenly realize you don't know what you're going to do next, you will fall right out of the zone.

This can easily happen when you are writing a book and suddenly realize that you never planned out or researched the next chapter.

More Reflections

Write your thoughts on these reflection questions in your Stop Procrastination Journal.

1. Do you think you have ever achieved a true flow state? If you have, do you remember the details? Do you remember how you achieved it? Can you replicate the process?
2. Has there been a time when you tried to achieve a flow state, but were unable to do so? Do you have any insight into what it might have been that stopped you from doing so?
3. How will you try to get into the zone for your next project?

---

[1] HTTPS://WWW.PSYCHOLOGYTODAY.COM/BLOG/BRAIN-WISE/201209/THE-TRUE-COST-MULTI-TASKING

7
"CHEAT" YOUR WAY OUT OF PROCRASTINATION

I bet reading the title of this section got you pretty excited. There are all these statements in our culture about suffering and sacrifice. A project only really counts if you suffered along the way.

But why on Earth would you want to live like that? I don't need you to suffer. I would much rather you enjoy every step of the journey. Do you think I could write this fast if I hated it?

What looks like cheating to other people can become the core of your anti-procrastination regime. Here are a few types of cheating that might work for you:

- Taking frequent breaks
- Listening to music in the background
- Listening to television in the background
- Taking regular naps
- Giving yourself rewards
- Playing video games while other people work

You probably get the idea now. Cheating is about doing things that most people think are bad ideas. Some of these are counterintuitive, but they can work for you. I use all of these techniques as part of my process.

Most of the rules you learned in school were designed to turn you into a drone. But that is not what you were meant to be. Drones procrastinate because they live joyless lives. You deserve better.

This book has one goal - to help you stop procrastinating. Any cheating that helps you achieve this goal counts as a win for me. I listen to music all the time while I'm working. Depending upon the type of work, I listen to different music and even watch television for some tasks.

For some work, I need music with no words so that I don't get distracted. Experiment with different styles of cheating to find the one that works best for you.

Journal

Below are some reflections on how "cheating" can help. Make sure to write your answers in your Stop Procrastination Journal.

1. Have you used "cheating" tactics in the past? Did they help you or make your procrastination worse?
2. Have you stopped yourself from cheating because it feels like it's against the rules? Do you feel like hard work should be hard?
3. Do you think that "cheating" could work for you? Or will it just bring too much distraction into your life?
4. Are you willing to give cheating a try? Why or why not?

8

HEALTH AND PROCRASTINATION

Health problems can destroy productivity. Earlier this week I had a major scare with my eyes. Paranoia turned into a case of Munchausen's, and I started to think I was going blind. Fortunately, my eye doctor was able to give me the right medicine to turn things around.

Getting your work done doesn't seem that important when you are dealing with real medical problems.

Procrastination and your health can end up in a vicious cycle if you allow them to turn against you. You can't work because you're sick, so you get stressed about work, so you don't want to work, so you procrastinate more, you get more behind, get more stressed, and your illness gets worse.

That's the worst merry-go-round in the world. Better to hop off it immediately.

There are three key ways that procrastination and your health interact.

1. Stress

According to a massive study published in the Public Library of Science Journal in February of 2016, "procrastination was consistently associated with higher stress, more depression, anxiety, fatigue and reduced satisfaction across life domains, especially regarding work and income."[1]

2. Avoiding the Doctor

When my eyes were acting up earlier this week, I thought about waiting a month to see my preferred doctor. I'm traveling, and at first, I thought seeing a doctor out of town would be a big hassle. Usually, I fly to Thailand when I want to see the doctor. But I realized I was procrastinating, and a good doctor now is way better than a great doctor in a month.

Most people have done this one. We start to feel sick, think that it might be something really serious, but we decide it's better not to know. We wait as absolutely long as possible before going to the doctor. It's better to think you're dying but not be sure, than to get that scary confirmation from your doctor.

If you have a health problem, it's always better to deal with it fast. Either you find out that nothing is wrong or you can start tackling the problem head on sooner. The sooner you catch most problems, the easier they are to treat.

3. Happiness

The Procrastination Research Group at Carleton University in Canada asked 2,700 people one question. "To what extent is procrastination having a negative impact on your happiness?"

Nearly half of the respondents (46%) admitted that procrastination hurt their happiness "very much" or "quite a bit."[2]

It's not a surprising result. Nobody thinks of procrastination as a good thing. The study on stress also found that procrastination leads to depression.

As someone who has suffered from depression, I can tell you that it damages your soul as it grinds you down.

Procrastinaion Cycle

There is a danger that procrastination and your health can enter into a vicious cycle. You start to suffer from health problems because of procrastination, then you avoid going to the doctor, so you get sicker, and the problem keeps growing.

Take your health seriously. Your mind, body, and spirit are all intertwined, and you must take care of all three. If your health suffers, delivering a project a few days late no longer seems that important.

Reflections

1. Has procrastination affected your health? Take some time to think about this, as you have probably never thought about this before.

2. Have you ever put off dealing with a medical condition or going to the doctor? What were the consequences? Did the doctor scold you for taking too long to come in?

3. Have you put off changing to a healthier lifestyle? Do you think it's worth the effort?

4. What will you do in the future to ensure that procrastination doesn't affect your health?

5. Did anything in this chapter surprise you? Have you thought about health, stress, and happiness in this way before? Do you need to make some changes in your life?

6. Are you procrastinating about a health issue right now? Be honest! Do you need to start exercising or to change your diet? How will you take action?

. . .

[1] http://journals.plos.org/plosone/article?id=10.1371/journal.pone.0148054

[2] https://www.procrastination.ca/media/

9

YOUR PHYSICAL ENVIRONMENT

I've touched on infrastructure at a few points in this book. Now that you have a deeper understanding of procrastination let's look a little deeper.

How would you feel if someone stood next to your desk eight hours a day, shouting at you while you tried to work?

It would be pretty hard to get things done! Imagine how much easier work would be the day after that person was fired. Removing physical elements from your life can often lead to a removal of procrastination.

Many people find that their productivity improves after canceling cable, selling the television or throwing out their video games.

The World Around You

There are a few other ways your physical environment can affect your procrastination:

1. If your working area is messy and disorganized, you are more likely to procrastinate.

2. If you do not have your materials organized in a way that makes sense to you, you are more likely to procrastinate.

3. If you do not have the materials you need readily at hand, you are more likely to procrastinate.

4. If you do not have a working environment that allows you to work smoothly and without interruption, you are more likely to procrastinate.

Do any of these problems sound familiar?

When I was in high school, like every other teenager in the world, my room was a disaster. You had to move things around just to walk from one side to the other.

This disorganization began to affect the quality of my work. When my room is messy, my mind feels messy, and I find it hard to work. Now I'm obsessed with having a clean work environment.

I have an office setup in the corner of my bedroom, and we clean the entire room at least once a day. With two young children, you can't wait any longer. When the room is messy, I still find it hard to focus in the way that I need.

Does a messy environment ever distract you?

Exercise

It's time to evaluate your work environment and find anything that is hurting your productivity or causing you to procrastinate. Write down your observations in your journal.

Take a good evaluative look at your work environment. Do you see any problems with your current setup? Are there people or distractions that are just too close? Be honest and be thorough.

Once you have made a comprehensive list of all the problems in your environment, organize and prioritize them. Focus on the biggest problems first and work your way down. Which factor do you need to deal with first?

Make a plan to carry out the changes that are required. Then enact that plan. In a few days, crack open your journal and answer the following questions:

. . .

1. Have you noticed an increase in your productivity? Is the desire to procrastinate getting smaller? Have you found yourself wanting to procrastinate less frequently?

2. Are there any additional changes you need to make to your workspace?

3. Do you have a plan for improving your environment even more?

10

MEDITATION

Meditation is a powerful tool that we can use to battle against procrastination.

Most people know the idea of meditation, but have never actually tried it. There are many different ways to experiment with meditation, and you might just find that one of these methods is perfect for you.

Meditation is a state of mind where you push away all those distracting thoughts. It's another way of getting into the zone. When I'm surfing or doing yoga with my wife, I don't have time to think about anything else that I'm doing. I can't think about work while I'm catching a wave.

With proper meditation, you are absolutely in the moment. A state where distractions fade away.

Raw meditation involves intense focus and a high degree of mindfulness. Mindfulness is the state of mentally living entirely in the present, giving absolutely no attention to the past or the future. It's the new name for "living in the moment."

There are several reasons why meditation is useful in the fight against procrastination:

- Mindfulness and distraction are mutually exclusive. They cannot both exist in your mind at the same time. When you are mindful, accomplishing tasks becomes easy.
- Meditation will increase your mental discipline, and you will effectively push aside distracting thoughts and strengthen your ability to focus.
- Meditation gives you an enhanced sense of peace. This is not just while you are meditating, but in your life overall.
- Meditation will make you a clearer and more decisive thinker. You will get more in touch with your inner thought process. You will more effectively and objectively understand your tendency to procrastinate, and learn how to overcome it.
- There are some great guided meditations, and I have links to them on the procrastination page of my website. Guided meditations will not only relax and focus you but also give you special mental tools specifically designed for dealing with procrastination.

Meditation Methods

1. Guided meditation

A guided meditation is usually relaxing music accompanied by a voice that takes you on a journey. This soothing voice calms your soul and guides you through the meditation process. This is a great place to start as a meditation beginner.

2. Mindfulness meditation

While all forms of meditation tend to support mindfulness, there are particular kinds of meditation that are designed to increase your mindfulness. An example of a basic mindfulness meditation is the following:

- Focus on your breathing and the sequence of its mechanics.
- Slowly but surely cultivate a focus that is entirely centered on the present moment
- Focus on the information that is coming in through your senses. What do hear, see, and smell at this present moment? Focus on nothing else.
- If any thoughts of the past or future come into your mind, ignore them and simply let them flow through your mind. Do not pay them any attention.

3. Visualization

Visualization is usually about imagining a beautiful scene within your mind. You begin with close and mindful attention to your breathing. Then you visualize yourself on a seashore, in the mountains or next to a beautiful lake. Try to imagine every possible detail. The focus on creating details removes the distractions from your mind. You don't have time to be distracted because your mind is so focused on painting the perfect scene.

4. Mantra

I don't use every meditation technique, but I do use mantras a lot. I talk about my mantras the most when I'm discussing fear, but they can also be used to help you develop focus. A mantra is a word or phrase that you say at regular intervals during your meditation. Whenever you need to bring back your focus, you speak your mantra, and it helps you stay the course.

You can write your mantra or build a variation of this phrase.

You have absolute power over your destiny and are capable of greatness. Your focus is unstoppable. You are at one with the moment, and nothing can distract you from your path.

5. Candle staring

For some people staring at nothing is a challenge. Light a candle and stare into the flame. Fire is quite hypnotic and is a great meditation assistant.

6. Yoga

Yoga is more than just exercise; it is also a practice that centers the mind. This activity uses every single part of your body and leaves your mind no time to wander. When I was younger, I practiced martial arts. Now that I'm older, I enjoy yoga and practice nearly every day. I am by no means a master, but I find that a good yoga session cleanses my mind of much of my stress.

7. Painting

Maybe all this meditation nonsense is a little too much for you. That's ok. I have a solution for you. There are some amazing videos where you can watch a man paint beautiful scenes. Just watching him paint and talk about what he's creating is incredibly relaxing. I have some links to these videos on my website as well.

Exercises

Exercise One

1. Try at least two of the forms of meditation listed above. Once you have done so, answer the following questions in your notebook.

a) How easy did you find it to do this form of meditation? Did you enjoy it?

b) How useful was your session? Did it help to center and calm you?

c) Do you find this style of meditation effective for you? Do you think others will work better?

d) Will you continue to use this form of meditation? Why?
Exercise Two
Once you have found a form of meditation that works for you, practice it every day for two weeks. Then answer the reflection questions in your Stop Procrastination Journal:

1. Has meditation lessened your urge to procrastinate?
2. Why do you think that is? What specific elements of your meditation regimen have helped the most?
3. If your meditation practice hasn't lessened your procrastination, what do you plan on trying next?
4. What other benefits has meditation given you? Can you see it helping you into the future?

Additional Benefits of Meditation

Most people start meditation for reasons other than procrastination. There are many physical and mental benefits to this practice. A recent study found that "brief meditation training has beneficial effects on mood and cardiovascular variables."[1]

Meditation is good for both the mind and the body.

Here is a list of the psychological and physical benefits of meditation that is by no means exhaustive:

Psychological benefits of meditation

- increase your happiness
- sharpen your mind
- expand your consciousness
- improve your ability to keep problems in perspective
- fight anxiety
- improve your emotional stability
- grow your creativity
- increase your level of intuition
- boost your clarity of thinking

- magnify your sense of well-being
- hone your ability to focus
- support your emotional stability.

Physical benefits of meditation

- lower your blood pressure
- increase your energy levels
- bolster your immune system.
- promote the production of serotonin, boosting your mood

---

[1] HTTP://ONLINE.LIEBERTPUB.COM/DOI/ABS/10.1089/ACM.2009.0321

11

WHAT HAVE WE LEARNED?

We've covered a lot of ground in a very short amount of time, but I'm glad we shared this journey together. You may want to flip back to different chapters as you continue to wrestle with procrastination.

It's time to ask yourself a critical question - what have you learned about procrastination and the ways to fight it?

In chapters 1 and 2, we discussed what procrastination is, and how negatively procrastination can affect your life. In chapters 3 and 4, we learned about the causes of procrastination, as well as the importance of motivation. In chapters 5 and 6, we discussed the importance of self-discipline and goal setting. In chapter 7, we talked about the idea of "cheating" your way out of procrastination. In chapter 8, we talked about the link between health and procrastination. In chapter 9, we discussed how physical surroundings and conditions can cause or prevent procrastination. And finally, in chapter 10, we talked about how meditation can assist you in your fight against your tendency to procrastinate.

Procrastination can seem like an overwhelming monster, but now you have the tools to conquer this beast. I have changed from a guy who didn't get to walk across the stage for college graduation into the author of dozens of bestsellers. If I can learn to focus, anyone can!

I believe in you.

As always, if you email me I will reply to you. I get emails every day from people who want to see if this is the real deal. I love helping the members of my tribe, and you can find a host of free tools, resources, blog posts and podcast episodes at ServeNoMaster.com all designed to help you continue this journey.

TAKE THE QUIZ

Thank you for reading PROCRASTINATION.

You made it all the way to the end and I'm so proud of you!

You wouldn't believe how many people buy a book on procrastination and then never read it.

In case you missed it at the beginning, here is the comprehensive procrastination assessment tool.

https://servenomaster.com/procrastinate

ABOUT THE AUTHOR

Born in Los Angeles, raised in Nashville, educated in London - Jonathan Green has spent years wandering the globe as his own boss - but it didn't come without a price. Like most people, he struggled through years of working in a vast, unfeeling bureaucracy.

And after the backstabbing and gossip of the university system threw him out of his job, he was "totally devastated" – stranded far away from home without a paycheck coming in. Despite having to hang on to survival with his fingernails, he didn't just survive, he thrived.

In fact, today he says that getting fired with no safety net was the best thing that ever happened to him – despite the stress, it gave him an opportunity to rebuild and redesign his life.

One year after being on the edge of financial ruin, Jonathan had replaced his job, working as a six-figure SEO consultant. But with his rolodex overflowing with local businesses and their demands getting higher and higher, he knew that he had to take his hands off the wheel.

That's one of the big takeaways from his experience. Lifestyle design can't just be about a job replacing income, because often, you're replicating the stress and misery that comes with that lifestyle too!

Thanks to smart planning and personal discipline, he started from scratch again – with a focus on repeatable, passive income that created lifestyle freedom.

He was more successful than he could have possibly expected. He traveled the world, helped friends and family, and moved to an island in the South Pacific.

Now, he's devoted himself to breaking down every hurdle entrepreneurs face at every stage of their development, from developing mental strength and resilience in the depths of depression and anxiety, to developing financial and business literacy, to building a concrete plan to escape the 9-to-5, all the way down to the nitty-gritty details of teaching what you need to build a business of your own.

In a digital world packed with "experts," there are few people with the experience to tell you how things really work, why they work, and what's actually working in the online business world right now.

Jonathan doesn't just have the experience, he has it in a variety of spaces. A best-selling author, a "Ghostwriter to the Gurus" who commands sky-high rates due to his ability to deliver captivating work in a hurry, and a video producer who helps small businesses share their skills with their communities.

He's also the founder of the Serve No Master podcast, a weekly show that's focused on financial independence, networking with the world's most influential people, writing epic stuff online, and traveling the world for cheap.

All together, it makes him one of the most captivating and accomplished people in the lifestyle design world, sharing the best of what he knows with total transparency, as part of a mission to free regular people from the 9-to-5 and live on their own terms.

Learn from his successes and failures and Serve No Master.

Find out more about Jonathan at:
ServeNoMaster.com

BOOKS BY JONATHAN GREEN

Non-Fiction

Serve No Master Series

Serve No Master

Breaking Orbit

20K a Day

Control Your Fate

Breakthrough (coming soon)

Habit of Success Series

PROCRASTINATION

Influence and Persuasion

Overcome Depression

Stop Worrying and Anxiety

Love Yourself

Conquer Stress

Law of Attraction

Mindfulness and Meditation Ultimate Guide

Meditation Techniques for Beginners

I'm Not Shy

Coloring Depression Away with Adult Coloring Books

Don't be Quiet

How to Make Anyone Like You

Develop Good Habits with S.J. Scott

How to Quit Your Smoking Habit

The Weight Loss Habit

Seven Secrets

Seven Networking Secrets for Jobseekers

Biographies

The Fate of my Father

Complex Adult Coloring Books

The Dinosaur Adult Coloring Book

The Dog Adult Coloring Book

The Celtic Adult Coloring Book

The Outer Space Adult Coloring Book

The 2nd Celtic Adult Coloring Book

Irreverent Coloring Books

Dragons Are Bastards

Fiction

Gunpowder and Magic

The Outlier (As Drake Blackstone)

ONE LAST THING

When you turn the page, Amazon will give you the option to rate this book and share your thoughts on Facebook and Twitter. If you found value in this book, I would appreciate it if you would take a few seconds and click the FIVE STARS icon.

It might seem like nothing, but every single vote counts. Clicking that button shows me that you appreciate the effort that went into putting this book together and it helps me to provide for my family.

Without stars and reviews, you would never have found this book. Please take just five seconds of your time to support an independent author by leaving a rating.

Thank you so much!

Sincerely,
    Jonathan Green

ServeNoMaster.com

www.ingramcontent.com/pod-product-compliance
Lightning Source LLC
Chambersburg PA
CBHW062054280426
43661CB00087B/660